THE MISSING PEACE

SAM CHAN

"In his characteristically disarming style, Sam Chan tears through the wrappings and the trappings to expose the beating heart of Christmas and to show why our hearts might want a piece of it. Read this book at your own risk. It might just change your life."

REBECCA MCLAUGHLIN, Author of *Confronting Christianity*

"The world desperately needs what Sam Chan describes so well—the peace that only Jesus Christ provides. This is a book that will resonate with you, whoever you are."

GLEN SCRIVENER, Director of SpeakLife;
Author of *The Air We Breathe*

"Sam had me from the opening paragraph, with his trademark blend of humour, common sense, and depth. Who hasn't had moments when peace feels out of reach? Taking his cue from the original Christmas story, Dr Chan shows why a birth long ago offers new life—and lasting peace—today. This book is perfect for sceptics, believers, and everyone in between."

JOHN DICKSON, Historian; Author of *Bullies and Saints* and
Is Jesus History?; Host of the Undeceptions podcast

"Writing from the perspective of an Asian-Australian medical doctor and pastor, Sam Chan diagnoses the profound longing so many of us have for peace, and then, as he explains Christ's coming at Christmas, he prescribes the solution to this deeply troubling world. Timely, well-illustrated, unique and piercing, I will certainly be giving this book to friends and family this Christmas."

RICO TICE, Founder of Christianity Explored Ministries;
Author of *The Ultimate Christmas Wishlist*

The Missing Peace
© Sam Chan, 2025

Published by:
The Good Book Company

thegoodbook.com | thegoodbook.co.uk
thegoodbook.com.au | thegoodbook.co.nz

Unless indicated, all Scripture references are taken from the Holy Bible, New International Version. Copyright © 2011 Biblica, Inc. Used by permission.

All rights reserved. Except as may be permitted by the Copyright Act, no part of this publication may be reproduced in any form or by any means without prior permission from the publisher.

Sam Chan has asserted his right under the Copyright, Designs and Patents Act 1988 to be identified as author of this work.

Cover design by Drew McCall

ISBN: 9781802543247 | JOB-008256 | Printed in India

Contents

1. Why We Lie Awake   7

2. In Search of an Umpire   15

3. Not Another False Alarm   33

4. Seen, Loved, Safe   47

5. Christmas Is for *You*   59

CHAPTER 1

Why We Lie Awake

One night I was lying in bed, eyes closing, seconds away from falling asleep. But then I looked up. There it was. A big, hairy, scary spider. On the wall. Just above my head.

The best option is to catch and release the spider outside, rather than kill it. But these spiders are very fast. Catching and releasing is great in theory, but nearly impossible in practice. And I couldn't leave the spider alone. It was hovering only inches above my face. So I slowly snuck out of the bed, grabbed a flip-flop and swung at the spider as hard as I could.

THWACK!

I missed.

The spider slid down the wall and down the side of my bed and hurried underneath it.

Out of all the possible outcomes, this was the worst. At least, when the spider was on the wall, I could see it and know where it was. Now it was under my bed.

Lurking.

Hiding.

Plotting.

What if it came out in the middle of the night, while I was asleep, and crawled over my face? What if it nibbled on my ear? What if it crawled into my open mouth or nose?

There wasn't much sleep that night. You need to be at peace to fall asleep, and I had no peace—not with a big, hairy spider under my bed.

On the Wall or Under the Bed

It isn't always a hairy spider under the bed that robs us of peace and keeps us awake at night. There are heaps of other things too. Most of us know that feeling, once the lights are off, of lying awake with our brains whirring. All of us have some "spiders": things that worry us, that nag away at us, that we would like to change but can't, or that we know we need to deal with but avoid. Sometimes they're obvious, on the wall. Other times they're under the bed, but still there.

What is it that keeps you awake at night?

Maybe it's wars. There are always wars somewhere, but lately they've been getting closer to home. The war in Ukraine was unexpected. Surely, we thought, there'll never be another major land-based war in Europe after World War II. But we were wrong. When I was doing PhD studies in the USA, some of my classmates were from Russia and some were from Ukraine. I cannot fathom that they're now enemies fighting each other.

Ukraine is a long way from Australia, and yet life here still feels less safe. We're a sparsely populated nation floating around in the Pacific Ocean. We're neighbours to some major geopolitical players who have more military muscle than we do. When push comes to shove, we're not going to put up much of a fight. And even if things don't go down that path, lately in Australia we've suffered an endless cycle of deadly bushfires, dystopian rains, and dam-bursting floods. Whichever country you're reading this book in, I'm sure that right now you can think of your own equivalent concerns.

Meanwhile, politics seems more heated. I remember when most people in most Western countries were fairly apathetic about who to vote for and reasonably relaxed about the result. We said things like "Do we have to vote? Does it really matter? Both parties are much the same anyway." But now people are passionate about their politics and there's often a feeling of apocalyptic zeal for one party and a pathological fear and hatred of the other side. It feels like life and death now. Doomsday stuff.

If all that isn't bad enough, most of us feel poorer than we did, and our economies feel less certain. Throughout the West, inflation suddenly sky-rocketed. For a long time, prices were stable—we paid the same for milk, medicines, and mortgages. But no more. You can chart the increasing prices on a graph with a hockey stick. My wife and I now check our bank statements before we shop for groceries. It's a white-knuckle ride each month to make sure there's enough in the bank to pay the credit-card bills.

All those things are happening *outside* of us. There are a lot of spiders around. And that's before we ask what we are like *inside*. I'm sure many of us would describe our inner world with words such as tired, exhausted, restless, wandering, searching, uncertain, unsettled.

Each day, most of us are greeted by a neighbour or colleague asking, "How are you?" It's a standard greeting with a stock-standard reply: "Good!" ("Fine" is also an acceptable option.) But deep down, in our heart of hearts, we sometimes want to scream back, "I'm not doing well. I'm busy. I'm over-worked. I have deadlines I can't meet. My parents are ageing, and I don't know how to help. I'm worried about my kids / I'm worried about whether I'll have kids. I have aches. I have pains. I don't sleep well. I've been awake since 2 a.m."

Maybe you know that feeling. It's the feeling of wishing you had peace but finding it hard to locate.

And then, to make things even worse, there's one time of the year that's sure to multiply the reasons for feeling that way.

CHRISTMAS.

The Problem with Christmas

I know that Christmas is usually associated with fun, happy stuff like brandy, bonbons and bonuses. But, if you're like me, you find that Christmas also dials up the stress levels.

There are all the Christmas preparations (real Christmas tree or fake one?), diplomatic family negotiations (do we have to invite Uncle Roger?), and cooking the meal (which we always overcook). But there's also the fact that the Christmas season comes around as an annual reminder that, yes, *twelve months have gone by.*

Twelve months have passed, and war isn't (despite what John Lennon announced) over. I still didn't clean out the study/shed/attic. We still didn't have the neighbours over for a meal. I still didn't exercise as I promised myself I would.

Christmas is my annual reminder that one whole year has passed, but I'm *not* one year better for it. Nothing changed. I'm still the same person as I was last year. So I'm haunted by the nagging feeling: "Is this the best it's ever going to get?"

Even Better Than Happiness

But while Christmas can make peace feel further away, at the same time, according to the Christian tradition, Christmas celebrates the possibility of peace.

Just for a moment, imagine if, this Christmas, you could be full of peace. Imagine being able to lie in bed and not have worries crowding in as you close your eyes at night or open them in the morning. Imagine being able to tell your neighbour or work colleague that you're doing well, and really mean it. Imagine being able to look at the to-do list and the calendar and the coming year and feel... peace.

Imagine that! Because peace really is the solution to all our problems. Recently, in the West, we decided that the goal of life is *happiness*. But more and more studies show that our chase for happiness is actually part of what's making us exhausted and stressed. Instead, we should be looking for *peace*: not only the absence of anxiety or stress but the positive experience of living with everything—or at least, everything that matters most—in its right place.

But what would it take to experience that kind of peace? And what does Christmas have to do with it? I want to make this claim (it's what this whole book is about): *the Christmas story offers you peace.*

Most of us will be familiar with the basic contours of "the Christmas story". It's the story that our well-meaning but perhaps mildly annoying Christian friend tries to tell us every year, when we'd rather just eat the pudding. It's the story we sing in the familiar Christmas carols. It's the story that the local church spells out on its billboard in the form of a dad-joke-esque slogan: "Jesus is the reason for the season" or "Putting Christ back into Christmas".

But just for a moment, let me be that well-meaning but mildly annoying Christian friend and remind you of the core of the Christmas story:

On the original Christmas Day, about 2,000 years ago, a baby called Jesus was born.

That's it.

Christmas offers us peace because of this story.

Really?

How can that story—of a baby, born millennia ago—bring real peace to a real person's real life now?

That's what this book is about. And to answer that question, first of all we need to look at why peace is so hard to find and to keep.

CHAPTER 2

In Search of an Umpire

When I first met my future wife, Stephanie, dating was super easy because we seemed to have so much in common: "You like pizza? Me too!"

Then we got married.

And it turned out that we were different people with different views. We disagree over how to hang the roll of toilet paper. We quarrel about how to stack the dishwasher. We have our differences about how to hang the t-shirts on the laundry line (upside down, right way up, or folded over?).

And these are the tiny fights. Don't get me started on whether the toilet seat should stay up or down.

But *why* do we fight?

Partly it's because there's no rulebook for these issues. If we argue about, say, how many players there are on a side in basketball, we can refer to an official rulebook. But there's no rulebook for how to hang toilet paper, stack a dishwasher, or hang out t-shirts. So we fight.

If we argue about mathematics or measurements—what's the size of that square?—we can refer to an absolute, external, authoritative reference point. It's called a ruler. And if we argue in a game of football—did the ball go in or out?—we have an official umpire or referee who makes the call. But if there's no umpire, then we have to argue with or fight with our opponent to determine if the ball was in or out. If there's an umpire, their decision is what counts, not who wins the fight. Disagreeing with the umpire won't change the decision. Fighting won't change the call.

This is why umpires are a necessary part of professional sport. They prevent fights. Can you imagine a professional game with no umpire, where the players have to make their own calls on what's in or out? The game will descend into farce, then a brawl, and perhaps a riot. Umpires don't just make calls. Their presence prevents fights and makes peace possible.

But to return to hanging toilet paper, stacking dishwashers, and hanging out t-shirts, there's no external rulebook, and there's no external umpire to make the call. So we fight. Resolving disputes becomes a game of might versus might. Who's the biggest? Who can shout the loudest or argue the longest? Who's the most stubborn?

Two Birds, One Chip

What's true on a personal and fairly unimportant level also holds true at a far bigger and more significant one. Here's the thing: if there's no God, then when it really matters, there's no rulebook and no umpire to make the call on who's right and who's wrong.

If there's no God and we're merely a sophisticated species of animal, then we have to do things the same way that animals do. We have to fight. When two birds fight over the same chip, who's right and who's wrong? One bird says, "My chip!" The other bird says, "My chip!" Whose chip is it? In the end, the strongest bird is right. Whose chip is it? The one who wins the fight.

So when Russia invades Ukraine, who's right and who's wrong? Both sides say that they're right and that the other side is wrong. Russia says, "This is our land". Ukraine also says, "This is our land". And if there's no external reference point—no umpire—then this is essentially two birds fighting over a chip. So we try to create "umpires"—for example, the United Nations—but that never works as well as we hope (and, after all, such an umpire is actually just another bird saying, "I'll decide whose chip it is").

If there's no God, then the biggest, loudest, stubbornest player wins. We see this on world stage. We see it in the school playground. We see it in our offices and our homes. And so any peace we enjoy is always brittle and often broken.

Is there any way we can say that there is such a thing as right and wrong, rather than just "the strongest wins"?

Fair, Just, Merciful

It's in light of this that the Christmas story is good news, because what Christmas says is *There is a God*. There is a reference point. And therefore, there can be peace.

More specifically, the Christmas story says that 2,000 years ago, when God sent his Son, Jesus, to us as a baby, God sent his Son to be the umpire of the universe. In fact, this is the underlying theme of the Bible. Six centuries before Jesus was born, a messenger from God called Isaiah made this promise:

For to us a child is born,
to us a son is given,
and the government will be
on his shoulders.

And he will be called
Wonderful Counsellor,
Mighty God,
Everlasting Father,
Prince of Peace.
Of the greatness of his
government and peace
there will be no end.
He will reign on David's throne
and over his kingdom,
establishing and upholding it
with justice and righteousness.

(From the Bible book of Isaiah,
chapter 9, verses 6 and 7)

The prophet Isaiah, speaking on behalf of God, promised that, one day in the future, God would send his Son, born as a baby. This baby would grow up to set up a future kingdom. But this would be no ordinary kingdom. This kingdom would be fair, just, and merciful. It would be a kingdom of peace. Why? Because God's Son would be the ruler of this kingdom, and he would be the Prince of Peace.

How? In three ways. Jesus is...

... OUR UMPIRE

Jesus is the Prince of Peace because he's the one officially sanctioned by God, the Creator of the universe, to be our rulebook—our absolute, objective, authoritative, reference point, our umpire.

Isaiah hints at this when he says, "The government will be on his shoulders". Jesus will be the one who governs. Jesus makes the calls. And if there really is a loving, personal Creator of this universe—and if this God really did send his Son, Jesus, to be our rulebook, reference point and umpire... then there can be peace.

This is how Christmas offers us the peace that we long for.

At a meta level, Jesus is our umpire—our "Prince of Peace". He is the ultimate example of how to live as humans—of what's right or wrong, in or out, fair or unfair. But Jesus is also the one we can appeal to. He's our standard. He's our absolute, objective reference point.

... RIGHTER OF ALL WRONGS

As the perfect umpire, Jesus will right all wrongs.

Isaiah promised that Jesus would rule with "justice and righteousness". This promise sounds good—who doesn't want a world like that? But it sounds even better if we understand when and where Isaiah made this pronouncement.

When Isaiah made this promise, there wasn't much

peace for the tiny nation of ancient Israel in which he lived—and things didn't get better between Isaiah's day and Jesus' birth. Israel then was the doormat of the Middle East.

It was annihilated by the Assyrians (700s BC), conquered by the Babylonians (600s), oppressed by the Greeks (300s) and occupied by the Romans (60s). If the ancient geopolitical world was the English Football League, then ancient Israel were the perennial easy-beats, at the bottom of the table, getting relegated to a lower division year after year.

Ancient Israel reminds me of the little people who are given a voice in the popular, unofficial national anthem of Australia: a song called "What About Me?" sung by Moving Pictures in 1982 and repopularised by Shannon Noll in 2004. It pictures a little boy whom no one ever really notices, who's "pushed around, knocked to the ground", and a girl who works in a corner shop and never manages to find her dreams. And both want to shout, "What about me? It isn't fair". Others are always, they say, taking more than they give, and they never get their share. They are the little people, for whom life doesn't really work and who always get trodden on by others.

Ancient Israel were the little guys: repeatedly disrespected, conquered, oppressed and subjugated.

Their endless cry was the same one we cry today—for justice, fairness, peace. We might not be a conquered nation, but we have the same existential longings. That's why we sing, "What about me?" That's why we hate it when things aren't fair.

It's into this heartache of ancient Israel, and into ours today, that God has promised that Jesus, the Son of God, will one day set up and rule for ever a kingdom where there will be the peace, justice and fairness that we cry out for.

This means that bullies will get what they deserve. Wrongdoers will be exposed and brought to justice. Those who cause injustice—both the injustice we see in the news and that which we're sometimes victims of in our own lives—will stand before Jesus and answer to him for what they've done.

... OUR GUIDE
One of my favourite podcasts is called *Where Should We Begin?* with Esther Perel, a therapist. In a typical episode, married couples come to Esther Perel with their painful stories of conflict. By the end of the episode, these couples are on their way towards resolving conflict, finding some sort of agreement and reconnecting.

How?

The Missing Peace

What happens is this: left to themselves, the couples will continue to fight because by themselves they can't see what's right or wrong, what's wise and what's a bit dumb. But when they come to Esther, she becomes their external reference point, providing fresh wisdom, insight and guidance. She sees things that they can't see. She empowers them with understanding and equips them with new possibilities.

In the same way, Jesus sees things that we can't see. The prophet Isaiah promised that Jesus would be our "Wonderful Counsellor". In other words, Jesus can do perfectly for us in every way what Esther does for those couples. He gives us his wisdom, insight and guidance.

Jesus can do that because he knows us better than we know ourselves. Did you notice that the prophet Isaiah also calls Jesus the "Mighty God"? This is a massive claim. If it's true, then Jesus is the one who made us— who created and designed us. If it's true, Jesus knows us inside out. Jesus has planned a better version of us. Jesus will empower and equip us to become the person we need to be.

Once again, if there's no God and we're left by ourselves to be our own reference point, then there can be no such thing as peace. But if Jesus really is who the Bible claims he is, then the possibility of peace is real.

But wait. Even if we agree that we need an external reference point for the possibility of peace—an umpire, a counsellor—can't it be any religious leader? Any wise teacher? Or my Auntie Jemimah? Or my friend Jay? Or whatever works for me? Why does it have to be *Jesus*?

Here's why: because Jesus is unique.

God, Really

In life, some things exist because of convention. For example, in the UK people play "football" with their feet. In the USA, people play "football" with their hands! They're completely different games, but by convention both are called "football", and so both are "football", to different people.

Other things exist because of reality. For example, gravity exists because it's real.

God exists as reality, not convention. While many of us get to choose our prime ministers or presidents, we don't get to choose who God is. God exists, simply because he is God. And in the Bible, Jesus, in his adult life, did many things as evidence that he really is that God who exists. For example, he performed many miracles—healing sick people, raising dead people back to life, walking on water.

These miracles can be hard to believe. I get it. If there's no God, then miracles make no sense. Miracles should

The Missing Peace

not happen—*could* not happen. If there's no God, then nothing that does not fit the laws of nature should ever happen. But if there is a God, then miracles make sense. If there's a God, extraordinary things *should* happen.

The miracle that speaks loudest to me is when Jesus feeds thousands of people with only five small bits of bread and two small fish (like sardine sandwiches!). But I'm a trained medical doctor. I believe we should base our views on evidence. So how can I believe that Jesus could feed thousands of people with only a handful of food: that Jesus made something come from nothing?!

But actually, everyone, including you, believes that something once came from nothing. Whether or not we believe in God, we believe that this universe once came from nothing and that life once came from non-life.

If you don't believe in a God, then you don't believe that extraordinary things should ever happen. But extraordinary things—like the universe and life—*did* happen. Something did come from nothing.

When Jesus miraculously fed thousands of people, he produced something from nothing. In other words, he repeated what he did when he created the universe and life. And, if he's God, that makes perfect sense. God is the best explanation for the something-from-nothing of the universe and of life; and he is the best explanation for the something-from-nothing of feeding thousands with a few loaves and fishes.

In other words, Jesus is showing that he *is* the God who makes something from nothing. And in the same way that he once breathed life into a lifeless universe, he can give us his life, both in this life and the life to come.

If this is true, then Jesus is uniquely qualified to be our external reference point. He is the umpire of the universe. Not by convention. Not by preference. But in reality.

One of Us

Jesus is uniquely qualified to be the umpire in our lives not only because he *is* God but because he *knows* us.

Jesus is the umpire, but Jesus also knows what it's like to play the game. On the first Christmas Day, Jesus became one of us—a living, breathing human. He understands first-hand our lived human experience. He was a baby, so he knows what it's like to be dependent on others for basic human needs. He grew into an adult, and he knows what it's like to be tired, sore, lonely, angry, sweaty, smelly, teary, hungry, thirsty and heartbroken.

Jesus knows first-hand my human longing for peace. Jesus knows what I'm feeling. Jesus knows what I'm looking for. As the Creator God who lived as one of us,

Love *and* Justice

Jesus is uniquely qualified to know how to satisfy my cry for peace.

That's who Jesus *is*. But what is Jesus *like*? Well, as you read about his life on earth, you realise that he is incredibly loving and that he cares incredibly deeply about justice.

If there's only love but no justice, there can be no peace. Imagine a god, religion or teacher who practises only love but not justice: the religious equivalent of "You're all winners!" Wrongdoing, injustice, immorality—all would be greeted with a nod and a smile, or maybe a slight frown, but nothing more. Liars, cheats and crooks would get away with murder (literally). The victims would cry for justice but never find it. Love without justice does not bring peace.

But now imagine the opposite: a god, religion or teacher who practises only justice but no love—the religious equivalent of "You're all cancelled!" Those who don't fit in or make the moral grade will be called out, shamed and cut off. Those who make mistakes can never move beyond them. Mess up and you're out, never to return. There's no possibility of forgiveness. Justice without love doesn't offer us peace either.

But Jesus is full of both love *and* justice. There is such

a thing as right and wrong, as honour and shame, as wholeness and brokenness. There will be a day when people are held accountable. But there's also forgiveness for those who know they need it. We all mess up, but we don't need to stay messed up. Jesus' love enables us to be forgiven, and it empowers and equips us to be the person of righteousness, honour and wholeness that we want to be and God calls us to be.

Choosing a Babysitter

All this means that Jesus *is* the umpire. But it also means that it is *great* that Jesus is the umpire.

We don't get to choose whether there's a God or what he is like. But let's say that we could—that, in the same way that we can choose our version of football, we can choose our version of God.

Which God would you choose?

What qualities do you want from God?

An Australian Christian speaker once answered that question with something like "I would choose my God based on who I want to babysit my child."

That's a great way of looking at it, isn't it? First, it shows why it's great that there is a God, rather than nothing. Nothing can't be there for you. Nothing can't help you. Nothing won't love you.

But it also shows why it's great that there is *this* God, because not all the "gods" out there are known for their love, gentleness and kindness. From my Asian background, I know that many Asian deities are depicted as cruel, mischievous and capricious. And I remember from reading Greek mythology that many ancient Greek gods are shown to be immoral, dishonest and self-serving. I'm not sure I would want these gods babysitting my child.

Jesus is different. Jesus is known for his sacrificial love. He loves people so much that he chose to die on a cross as a selfless act of goodness for others. That's the kind of person I want to look after my child. I want God to be good, not only powerful. And in Jesus, I find that kind of God. The God who exists is the God whom I want to exist.

And it's only the *Christian* story that shows us that God goes out of his way to be good. It's only the Christian story that presents us with the God who became a human like us at the first Christmas, and who again and again went out of his way to be good. Here's just one example, from one of the Bible's Gospels (accounts of Jesus' life):

Jesus went to a town called Nain, and his disciples and a large crowd went along with him. As he approached the town gate, a dead person was being carried out—

the only son of his mother, and she was a widow. And a large crowd from the town was with her. When the Lord saw her, his heart went out to her and he said, "Don't cry."

Then he went up and touched the bier they were carrying him on, and the bearers stood still. He said, "Young man, I say to you, get up!" The dead man sat up and began to talk, and Jesus gave him back to his mother.

They were all filled with awe and praised God. "A great prophet has appeared among us," they said. "God has come to help his people." This news about Jesus spread throughout Judea and the surrounding country. (Luke 7:11-16)

In the same way that God once brought life from non-life into this universe, Jesus brought life into the non-living widow's son. Jesus showed that he *is* the God who created the universe and life.

But Jesus didn't *have* to do this miracle. There was no *ought* that was making him do anything. But he *chose* to do it. He went out of his way to help. Why? Because "his heart went out to her".

Jesus is God. And he's the *good* God. He loves us. He goes out of his way to care for us. He will do whatever it takes to offer us peace.

The Missing Peace

Remember, if there's no external umpire, there can be no peace. And the good news is that at the first Christmas, Jesus—God himself—arrived to be our umpire. But more than this, to have the peace that we wish for, we need that umpire to be someone we respect and whose verdicts we can welcome, even if we don't understand or instinctively agree with them; and the good news is that in his life, Jesus showed that he not only has power but that he cares—that he is good.

So Christmas declares that there is a God.

He's a God who cares about justice and love.

Therefore there can be peace.

But then, if God is powerful and loving and cares about justice... 2,000 years after he came, why is there still no peace?

CHAPTER 3

Not Another False Alarm

Years ago, Stephanie and I lived in Chicago, and our apartment block was right next to the local fire station and had a very sensitive fire-alarm system. This meant two things: first, that whenever anyone burned their cooking, the alarm went off; and second, that before anyone had time to call the fire department to let them know it was a false alarm, the fire trucks would be there.

It happened so regularly that both the apartment residents and the firefighters became numb to the whole thing. It was always going to be a false alarm.

So it was that one evening, my wife was in the kitchen cooking when sure enough, the smoke from our cooking set off our fire alarm. And *BOOM!* The firefighters came storming into our living room. Of course, they assumed it was another false alarm. "What have you been cooking?" they joked. There was no thought of evacuating the building. Instead, they hung around and chatted for a bit and then, after some high-fives, we all said bye, and they left.

Then I wandered into the kitchen.

Our saucepan was a charred, black shell of metal. The ceiling was covered in soot.

There had been a fire—a real fire—in the kitchen. A large oil fire that fortunately had burnt itself out.

We had all assumed that it was a false alarm. But this had been the real thing. The whole apartment block could have burnt down. *And it was our fault.* The problem was real. The problem was right in our own kitchen. The problem was *us*.

Whenever we hear any alarm—burglar alarm, fire alarm, car alarm—we tend to assume that it's a *false* alarm. We don't stop. We don't check. We continue doing what we're doing. In fact, we think it looks stupid to check. And even if it's a *real* alarm, we still don't stop because we think it's somebody else's problem. Besides, what can we do anyway?

But what if it's not a false alarm? What if it's real? And what if we're the ones at fault? And what if we have the responsibility to do something about it?

But what has any of this discussion of alarms got to do with Christmas?!

Everything.

What's in a Name?

Let's go back to the original Christmas story. Mary is pregnant, even though she's a virgin—pregnant with God's Son. Unsurprisingly, her fiancé, Joseph, doesn't feel great about this, so God sends an angel to him, who says this to him:

> *Joseph son of David, do not be afraid to take Mary home as your wife, because what is conceived in her is from the Holy Spirit. She will give birth to a son, and you are to give him the name Jesus, because he will save his people from their sins.*
>
> (Matthew 1:20-21)

When Steph and I were expecting our first child, we took a long time deciding what to name him. Part of the process involved going through the list of top-ten dog names, because my name, Sam, has been a top-ten dog name for decades. That year, the No. 1 dog name in Australia was Jack! Fantastic. "We will call our son Jack," we decided. "Jack is a strong name. Everyone loves Jack. That's why it's a top-ten dog name!"

Then we realised we couldn't call our son Jackie Chan. Unless he learned to fight as well as the real Jackie

Chan, he was going to be teased a lot. So instead, we named our son Toby—another top-ten dog name.

My Asian relatives were horrified: "You can't give your child a *dog name*!" That's because, in Asian culture, names have a meaning. You don't just choose a name from a list. The name is a message.

God may as well be Asian because this is exactly what he did. God deliberately chose a name with a meaning: Jesus. This baby's name was God's message to the world. God chose the name Jesus because Jesus literally means "the Lord saves". In this context, the angel explained to Joseph, it was a fitting name because Jesus would "save his people from their sins".

This is the meaning. This is the message. From God. To us, at the first Christmas.

Jesus coming to us as a baby was more than a symbol of God's love. It was more than a gesture of goodwill. It was to save his people from their sins.

What does that mean? The two key words are "save" and "sins".

The second word is God sounding the fire alarm.

The first word is God sending the fire brigade.

But Where's the Fire?

As we've already seen, there's a lot to be alarmed about *out there*.

And that's where the problem is, isn't it? Out there, not in here. I'm not the crazy president who invades countries. I'm not the politician who sparks culture wars. I'm not a shock jock. I'm not part of the crazy right or left. I'm not the virtue-signalling, trolling keyboard militant. I'm not the one behind the climate disasters—I recycle my garbage!

But the word "sins" isn't talking only about out there. It's talking about in here too. What I'm like—and what you're also like.

The original Copernican Revolution shifted humans from believing that the sun revolved around the earth to believing that it's the other way around—that the earth revolves around the sun. And here's another "Copernican Revolution" we need to undergo—from believing that the problem is only *out there* to believing that the problem is also *inside* all of us.

I'm the problem.

Aleksandr Solzhenitsyn is an example of someone who shifted. Solzhenitsyn was a Russian writer who, in the 1940s, criticised the Soviet leader, Joseph Stalin. As a result, he ended up in the Russian Gulag prison system for many years. In his writings, Solzhenitsyn described the horrible stuff that went on in the camps—beatings, starvation and deaths from the cold.

Solzhenitsyn had every right to hate his prison guards. It's a very simple logic. The prison guards were the bad guys, and the prisoners were the good guys. Solzhenitsyn was one of the good guys. But Solzhenitsyn went through his own "Copernican Revolution". He realised that the problem wasn't just *out there* in the prison guards, in the system, in Stalin's brutality. The problem was also *inside*—inside the heart of each and every person, including Aleksandr Solzhenitsyn. He was also the problem.

This led Solzhenitsyn to write in *The Gulag Archipelago*:

The line separating good and evil passes not through states, nor between classes, nor between political parties either—but right through every human heart—and through all human hearts.

Solzhenitsyn was claiming that every human person, no matter how good, has a streak of evil; and that every human person, no matter how evil, has a streak of good. And that means that each and every human is part of the problem.

This makes sense. In the end, the world is only the sum of its parts. And we're the parts that make up the world.

If this world is broken, it's because we're broken. If this world is messed up, it's because we're messed up. If this world is corrupt, it's because we're also corrupt. Or, as Solzhenitsyn reminds us, the problem isn't only out there. The problem is inside here—inside you and me.

Jesus said something similar:

Why do you look at the speck of sawdust in your brother's eye and pay no attention to the plank in your own eye? How can you say to your brother, "Let me take the speck out of your eye," when all the time there is a plank in your own eye? You hypocrite, first take the plank out of your own eye, and then you will see clearly to remove the speck from your brother's eye.
(Matthew 7:3-5)

The problem isn't just in other people. The problem is us. Which of us has never hurt someone else (with words if not with fists)? Never made someone cry? Never taken advantage of someone to get what we want? We ourselves are the problem—and we might be greater contributors to the brokenness of this world than we like to think.

What's Causing the Fire?

The word "sin" means different things to different people. When you hear the word "sin", you might think of some grumpy, old-school Bible-thumping preacher who screams and points at you and calls you a sinner—an authoritarian figure who imposes their outdated views of morality upon others. Or maybe when you hear the word "sin", you think of a so-called guilty or forbidden but entirely harmless pleasure—like chocolates, ice-cream or lingerie. Something to giggle about but not take too seriously.

So, what does the Bible mean by "sin"? What exactly is Jesus coming to save us *from*? Well, we can start to answer that question by first asking, "What is Jesus coming to save us *to*?"

According to the Bible, Jesus saves us from our sins to enjoy peace. If we start from here, then sin is the opposite of having peace. Sin is having things not in their right place. We will see this in our heart, thoughts, actions and relationships.

Many years ago, in my son's football team there was one boy who often broke the rules. His tackles were illegal. He started fights. He bad-mouthed the umpire.

He was guilty of breaking the rules. But that's not all that was wrong. He was out of sorts with himself. Deep down, he was profoundly unhappy. Maybe he was out of sorts with his friends and family. In this sense, there was brokenness in his life. And he was disrespecting the game. He was letting down his teammates. He was letting down his coach.

The Missing Peace

In many ways, sin is the same in our life. In a very simple sense, we can say it's breaking the rules that God has programmed into this universe. It's refusing to abide by his standards of right and wrong. But at a deeper sense, we're sinful because we're out of sorts with ourselves, our friends and family, and ultimately God. We don't honour, love or worship the God who made us and gives us life. We often let down our friends and family. Often we let ourselves down.

So sin is serious because it stops us being the best people we can be and it adversely affects those around us. And ultimately the *most* serious aspect of sin is that it cuts us off from God. In the same way that a leaf separated from its tree is cut off from its life-giving source, our sin means that we are cut off from the God who made us and gave us life. We're already "dead" in this life because we're living it without God; and after death, we'll be truly dead, with no chance of a future life with God—an experience of endless, eternal darkness, of separation from God.

This is sin. And so our sin is the reason why we don't experience the peace we long for and were designed to enjoy—peace with ourselves, peace with others and peace with God.

So when the angel uses the word "sins" as he speaks to Joseph, it's a fire alarm for us to heed. Jesus' birth and

Jesus' name warn us of danger. Real danger. The danger is the sin in our hearts.

We're All Not Doing Okay

Back when I was a university student, I'd often eat with a group of friends at a restaurant. At the end of the meal, every one of us paid what we thought we should pay.

Somehow, the amount of money in the middle of the table was always short. It was never enough—yet every one of us was convinced that we had paid exactly what we should pay. I always knew *somebody* needed to put in more money, but I also always knew that that somebody was not me. I owed nothing.

Looking back now, I'm convinced that in reality we were *all* short. Each of us paid less than we should. That's because we were university students, on limited budgets, trying to pay only what we had to pay and not a dollar more. I think that each of us probably also overlooked the hidden costs of the meal—drinks, surcharges, taxes, etc. And so each of us was short.

In the same way, we all fall short of who we're supposed to be—by our own standards, our family's standards, our friends' standards and, ultimately and most importantly, by God's standards. We should be better. We might think we're doing okay, but the reality is that we're really not. Paul, a follower of Jesus, explains it this way in the Bible:

All have sinned and fall short of the glory of God.
(Romans 3:23)

This is humbling, confronting and unpleasant. Christmas asks us to examine ourselves. Can we admit that inside our hearts we will find pain, hurt, regret, brokenness, secrets, skeletons, guilt and shame?

We're not thoroughly evil. But we're also not thoroughly good. The line that divides good and evil exists inside my heart, and it exists inside your heart. The reason for our lack of peace begins inside our hearts.

The Message We Need

Now we can see how Christmas is God's "fire alarm" for us: the baby's name is Jesus because "he will save his people from their sins". We need saving *from* our sin— our falling short of God's standards.

But Jesus' name is not only a fire alarm for us—it's also a promise of rescue from the fire. Jesus didn't come just to show and tell us how to live. Jesus came to *save* us. Our chief *problem* is sin and the separation from God that brings. Therefore our chief *need* is to be rescued from our sins and restored to relationship with God. And Jesus' chief purpose in being born was to do exactly that.

Our No. 1 need is not for more money, more possessions, or more holidays. Our No. 1 need is for somebody to save us from our sins. Until we address this, we won't get to the root of the problem, and we will find everything else we gain or gather to be frustratingly unsatisfying.

I think this is a ripe moment to hear this message. The late 20th-century was filled with optimism. All we needed were more medicines, more science, more money, better education and good government, and we were on our way to a better world. Nothing was going to stop the juggernaut of Progress!

But this dream crashed like a tower of Jenga bricks. In the 21st century, wars grumble on. Politics are dysfunctional. Our society is deeply divided. Family meals end in culture-war arguments. And... we have had a pandemic, with more pandemics predicted to come.

Medicine, science, money, education, government, as good as they are, have not been enough. We need something or somebody else who will get to the root of our human problem—sin—and provide a solution.

Maybe this isn't the Christmas message we want to hear. But it's the Christmas message we *need* to hear. Enter Jesus. Enter Christmas. Enter God's solution to our problem.

An Annual Intervention

It was the summer holidays. I was about ten and my brother would have been eight. Summers back then were the stuff of boyhood dreams. No homework. No school. No exams. Instead, my brother and I had long, endless summer days of pure fun—outdoors, bicycling, playing cricket. What could go wrong?

One night, Mum and Dad pointed out to us that we had not showered for five straight days. It was an intervention. Had Mum and Dad not interrupted our cycle of fun, I'm not sure we would ever have showered. We were clueless. Oblivious. Too used to our own filth.

And maybe that's why Christmas comes once a year. It's God's annual intervention. An interruption to our cycle of work, rest and play. Without Christmas, we might not see our need for peace because we've become oblivious to our own brokenness, blemishes and blame.

Interventions are always awkward. This one is no different. It's not easy to admit that you're a sinner. It's a humbling word to hear.

But Jesus himself said that he didn't come to save good people. He didn't come to save nice people who think they're okay with God. He came to save humble people—those who can admit to themselves and to him that they need to be saved from their sins:

> *It is not the healthy who need a doctor, but those who are ill. I have not come to call the righteous, but sinners to repentance. (Luke 5:31-32)*

> *For all those who exalt themselves will be humbled, and those who humble themselves will be exalted.*
> *(Luke 14:11)*

Christmas is God's explicit message to us. The Son of God has come to us as a baby called Jesus. Why? Because we have sinned, and because he will save us from our sins. Because we are the reason why we have no peace, and because he has come to restore us to that peace.

So, what does having that peace, in a world that is still not at peace, look like in our actual lives?

CHAPTER 4

Seen, Loved, Safe

If you are anything like me, one of the least peaceful aspects of Christmas is buying presents for your friends and family.

Our extended family finally declared a truce a few years ago. We agreed that there would be no more present-giving, and everyone in the family breathed a sigh of relief. No more hunting in bargain shops in the final chaotic days before Christmas.

But, as a husband, I still need to buy a present for Steph. Every Christmas. Every year. This is my duty. This is my calling. This is my time to shine… or fail.

So every year, I try hard. I do my research. I listen out for hints. I take advice. I find something that I am sure Steph will both want and need.

Every year, it turns out that Steph neither wants nor needs what I've given her.

Except last year. Last Christmas, I gave Steph a robot vacuum cleaner. Other than that it was as much a gift to me as it was to her (since we both do the vacuuming), what's not to love about a robot vacuum cleaner?

She hated it.

Until... a few months later, she tried it out. She was stunned by how good it was. No more vacuum-cleaning for her (or for me). Steph loves it. She's nicknamed it "Robby", the robot vacuum cleaner.

This was a spectacular win for me. I now like to point out to Steph that I know her better than she does. Why? Because I didn't simply get her a gift she needed. I got her a gift she needed *and didn't know she needed*.

That is *great* husband-ing.

That robot vacuum cleaner filled a metaphorical hole in my wife's life that she didn't even know she had. It filled a *vacuum* in her life (sorry).

We all have holes (metaphorically) that need filling. We all have things we know we need—and, perhaps, things we need without knowing it.

And the first Christmas was the moment when God, the greatest gift-giver, reached down to this world in

How Are You... Really?

As a medical doctor, I (and other doctors) make fun of our colleagues who are psychiatrists or psychologists and who work as counsellors. We joke that it doesn't take much training to be a counsellor. You only need to ask two questions...

"How are you doing?"

And...

"How are you *really* doing?"

Let me ask you the same thing.

How are you doing?

How are you *really* doing?

If we're honest, we will say there's a hole in our life. We're missing something. But we don't quite know what it is.

So we keep wandering.

Searching.

Trying to fill that hole with things like work, relationships, experiences, chasing success, owning stuff...

But the hole is still there.

So we work harder, pursue a relationship (or change a relationship), seek new experiences, chase more success and own more stuff...

But the hole is still there.

Maybe that's partly why we're so stressed, tired and restless. We keep searching. We keep chasing. We keep filling that hole with things that simply can't fill it. The hole is still there.

So what will fill that hole? What is it that we need?

To answer this, let's change the question slightly. What does a *child* need? Besides the basic needs—food, water, shelter, sleep—what does a child really need?

Child psychologists basically agree that a child essentially needs three things: to be seen, to be loved and to know they're safe. That's it.

When I used to take my young children to the park to play, at first I took a book. I thought this was an opportunity to relax. I was wrong. My children wanted to be *seen*. Every second, they called out, "Dad! Dad! Dad!" Or "Watch me!" or "Did you see me?" If my eyeballs briefly wandered to my book, the call would go up again: "Dad! Dad! Dad!" A child psychologist tells me that my job as a parent is to yell pre-emptively "Look at you!" My children need to know I see them. Once they know they're seen, I see the delight on their faces. Only then can they enjoy their play in the park.

A child also needs to be *loved*. This seems obvious. But a child needs to know that they're loved *unconditionally*. It's always a wrong move as a parent to hint that your love is conditional, dependent on how your child performs at school or in sport. Children need to know that they're loved unconditionally. Once they know they're loved no matter what, they thrive because they know that they have the permission to excel but also the freedom to fail.

A child also needs to know that they're *safe*: physically, psychologically and relationally. If a family suffers the misfortune of job loss, change of housing, divorce or death, it can be difficult for a child to feel safe. In these cases, the job of a parent is to show a child that, despite these unforeseeable uncertainties, the parent's love for their child is still 100% certain. It's unconditional. Children can find safety in a parent's love for them. That is a rock-solid foundation in their life.

I don't think we ever outgrow these three needs: to be seen, to be loved, to be safe.

If I Couldn't See My Dad...

Beckham is a Netflix docuseries that follows the life of David Beckham, the global football star, who once played for Manchester United. In one episode we reach the 1999 European Champions League final. If Beckham and his team win, they'll achieve a never-before-achieved, almost impossible sporting achievement: the Treble of the English Premier League, English FA Cup, and Champions League trophies.

Before the match starts, the players line up and face the crowd of 100,000 people. This is high sporting drama. Here's how Beckham describes it:

> *"When the teams were lining up ... I was searching for [my fiancée] Victoria and my mum and dad."*

His teammate Gary Neville adds:

> *"Our parents were never not there. But I remember looking up, and this stadium's vast. If I couldn't see my dad, something would have been missing. It unnerved me. The same with David, with his mum and dad in the stand. Seems ridiculous when you're a 23-year-old football player, but it became more of a comfort blanket. They're there. They're watching."*

Beckham agrees:

> *"As soon as I saw them, I was ready."*

These are hugely successful, very confident football players who do this for a living. But they need to know that Mum and Dad are watching. They find safety in knowing that they're seen and loved. Only then can they happily play football.

It's the same for us. We never outgrow these needs—to be seen, to be loved, to be safe.

This is the hole in our life, and until we fill this hole, we will be restless. Wandering. Searching. Anxious.

Perhaps you're still trying to fill that hole with things that don't fill it—striving to succeed, to prove yourself, to own more things. But the hole in life remains, and until the hole is filled, there can be no peace.

This is why we need to revisit the original Christmas story and hear what it promises us.

The Promise of Christmas

When Jesus was born in a small town called Bethlehem, a throng of angels announced the news to a bunch of working-class shepherds who were working in nearby fields. It was night. The shepherds were camped out in the fields to watch over their sheep. It was a cold, dirty, smelly sort of job, unpleasant and low-paying. Not many Bethlehem parents were wanting their children to grow up to be shepherds or to marry a shepherd.

Yet it's to these shepherds that God sent his angels to announce great news. We find the angels' message in the pages of the Bible:

Glory to God in the highest heaven, and on earth
peace to those on whom his favour rests. (Luke 2:14)

This is a stunning promise: of God's peace and favour. It deliberately recalls an ancient blessing that the prophet Moses gave to God's people thousands of years earlier:

The LORD bless you
and keep you;
the LORD make his face shine on you
and be gracious to you
the LORD turn his face towards you
and give you peace. (Numbers 6:24-26)

This blessing has now been fulfilled by the coming of Jesus, the Son of God, as a baby born in a manger in Bethlehem. The shepherds heard it first. And now it's our turn—*your* turn—to hear it. God, through the angels and his prophet Moses, has promised to fill the hole in our life. God will give us peace. We can stop searching. Stop wandering. No longer restless, we find our rest in God.

Somehow, in Jesus, we will be seen by God. Loved by God. Safe in God. The Treble.

God will do this by giving us his "face". As an Asian, I'm from a shame-honour culture, so I understand this language of "face". In shame-honour cultures, the opposite of "shame" is "face". If your parents turn away their faces, then you're covered in shame. But if they turn their faces towards you, then you're honoured. You're loved. You're safe.

There's an echo of that when David Beckham and his Manchester United teammates desperately search a crowd of 100,000 and try to see the *faces* of their mums and dads. If they can see their faces, then they know they will be okay.

God promises that he will "turn his face" towards us. He will "make his face shine" upon us. We're going to be okay if we know that no matter what happens, we're seen by God, loved by God, and safe with God.

This is where our peace comes from.

How to Be Seen, Loved, Safe

Of course, being seen, loved, and safe only matters if it comes from someone significant in our life. We don't care whether a random stranger sees us. But we do care whether our father does. That's why, in the end, God's promise only comes to fulfilment if *he* becomes that most significant loved one in our life—if it's *his* face that we most want to know is smiling on us.

That's how Christmas works. In Jesus, we can have a personal relationship with God, as our loving heavenly Father. When we make Jesus our King, God is not a random stranger. He is no longer just the maker or judge of this universe. He is now our heavenly Father. Through Jesus, we have a personal relationship with God, not just now but for ever. And this means our most basic needs—to be seen by, loved by, and safe with God—can be met, both in this lifetime and the life to come.

This is peace.

Finding *Tsong*

There are two sides to the peace Jesus offers.

First, there is what Jesus removes from us. He washes away our sins. He bears them for us, along with all the shame, pain, hurt, regret, brokenness and guilt that accompany them. He takes the separation from God they deserve. When he died, Jesus saved us from our sins and their eternal consequences, just as his name says he would.

The second side of peace is what Jesus gives us. God will give us his favour, face and forgiveness. Through Jesus, we enjoy a loving, personal relationship with God. We have a restored relationship with God—we are seen, loved, safe… we are saved by God.

I love doing puzzles: jigsaws, sudokus, crosswords. I get an amazing feeling when I complete a puzzle. When that last jigsaw piece snaps into place, when the last number completes the sudoku grid, or when the last word completes the crossword, it's an amazing feeling of *aaaarrrrhhhh*. (I'm not sure any real English word captures this satisfying moment.) There's a sense of calm, delight and euphoria. Everything is in its right place. Everything is where it should be.

My Cantonese father describes this as *tsong*. The ancient Greeks called it *eudaimonia*. The ancient Hebrews used the word *shalom*. And perhaps the closest modern English word we have is "peace". Everything is in its happy place; everything is exactly where it should be.

Wholeness. Fulfilment. Restoration. Completeness. Wellness. Balance. Beauty.

Tsong. Eudaimonia. Shalom.

Peace.

This is the peace that the angels announced and that we can experience on earth now that Jesus has arrived.

This is not peace on earth in the sense of an instant end to wars, pain and poverty. Instead, it's peace on earth "to those on whom his favour rests". When you know that Jesus has taken your sin so that you now enjoy God's favour, then you can navigate the wars and pain and poverty and whatever else this broken world throws at you, and you can do it with a sense of peace because you're at peace with God.

Here Is What We're Looking For

This means we have all the ingredients in this life to survive and thrive. God rests, refreshes and restores us. God empowers us to flourish in our relationships, work, music, sport and play. God knows us personally; and we know him personally.

Everything is in its right place. Everything is where it should be. Even more importantly, *you're* where you should be.

Jesus hints at this when he gives us this invitation:

Come to me, all you who are weary and burdened, and I will give you rest. Take my yoke upon you and learn from me, for I am gentle and humble in heart, and you will find rest for your souls. For my yoke is easy and my burden is light. (Matthew 11:28-30)

With Jesus, we will have rest for our souls. In Jesus, we will find our peace.

CHAPTER 5

Christmas Is for *You*

When our baby son turned one year old, Steph and I threw a big birthday party for him. We invited all our friends and family. It was a big affair. We put a lot of work into it.

Well, truth be told, Steph put a lot of work into it. I did not. That's because I'm sceptical about birthday parties for one-year-olds. Do they really know what a birthday party is? Do they even know that this party is for *them*?

Then my wife brought out the birthday cake, and we gathered around my son and sang, "Happy Birthday".

My son's face brightened. He smiled the biggest smile he'd ever smiled. He squealed with laughter.

Wow!

Somehow my son knew that this was *his* day. This party was for *him*.

It's the same for us. Christmas is a big affair. It's a national holiday. It's a highlight of the year.

But what's it actually *for*?

I'm writing this book to tell you that Christmas is *your* day. All this fuss is for *you*.

Remember that when Jesus was born, angels announced the news to shepherds. I quoted it earlier, but I left out what the angel said right at the beginning of the message:

> *Today ... a Saviour has been born to you. (Luke 2:11)*

Don't miss that. In one sense, the whole reason that Christmas exists is you. You are the reason for the season. Jesus came to offer you the opportunity to be seen, loved and safe in the eyes of the only person whose opinion matters eternally.

God Knows

God loves you so much that he changed the trajectory to send you his Son, Jesus, born as a baby in Bethlehem.

God knows that you struggle to find peace in life and that you aren't at peace with him. God knows that the only possibility of peace is if his Son, Jesus, comes into the world to be your Prince of Peace. God knows that the root problem is your heart—your sin. That's why God sent Jesus to save you.

This is the double edge to the Christmas story.

So how should we respond? On the one hand, you need to admit that you're the reason why Jesus comes into your world: that he came to save you from *your* sins. But, on the other hand, you can rejoice that Jesus chose to come to save you. In Jesus, you can have a new start. You can become part of a new kingdom in which Jesus is your Prince of Peace. That peace begins in your heart, and it's a peace that radiates into all your life—to your friends, family, and ultimately the world.

How to Opt In

"Peace on earth" is a real thing. I know because I've experienced it. But it's not automatic. We have to opt in to have this peace. Our default position is to live without peace, without Jesus, trapped in our endless cycle of exhaustion, anxiety, stress, feeling *bleh*. For as long as we stay in that place, Christmas will be our yearly reminder that nothing has changed. And worse, it'll be an annual reminder that we're one year closer to our eternal destiny. The worrying thing about no peace is not only our struggle on this side of death but things being even worse on the other side of death.

But we have a better choice. We can opt in to peace. We do this by choosing to receive God's Christmas gift of Jesus. We will be saved from our sins. We will discover the true peace that comes from a personal relationship with God. In Jesus, we will be seen, loved, and safe with God. This is a peace we enjoy with God both in this life and the life to come, living in a world of peace and justice and love, with God, for ever.

So how do you opt in to this peace? How do you receive God's gift of Jesus?

A simple way is to do the ABCs:

Admit... your need for Jesus to save you from your sins. You have guilt, shame, brokenness, hurt, regret.

Believe... that Jesus really did come to save you from your sins.

Commit... to Team Jesus. Bend the knee. Become loyal to Jesus as your Prince of Peace. Join his kingdom. Embrace his mission to bring mercy, justice and love.

Wherever you are right now as you read these words, why don't you call out to God and talk to him about these ABCs? You can pray in your heart or out aloud to God. Humble yourself and admit your need for Jesus. Ask Jesus to save you from your sins. Acknowledge your newfound loyalty to Jesus.

The Missing Peace

God will hear. God will fill you with Jesus' Spirit. God will give you the fresh start that you're looking for.

If you do this, you will also enjoy D:

Delight... in what God has done for you. Taste the joy of knowing God's peace, in this life and the life to come.

Do this, and the endless cycle of stress, anxiety and feeling *bleh* will be broken. You'll have a fresh start. God will shine his face upon you. You will taste God's "favour".

With Jesus as your forgiving King, Christmas stops being a nagging, annual reminder that a year has passed and the fundamental direction of your life still isn't sorted—instead, Christmas becomes a joyful yearly promise that, because Jesus was born to save us from our sins and to give us peace, we don't need to worry about the "spiders" in our lives—not even death. Now you can enjoy the season, enjoy the next year, and walk through all the ups and downs and joys and challenges all your life, knowing that you are seen, loved and safe... that you have peace with God.

Thanks for reading this book. We hope you enjoyed it and found it helpful.

Most people want to find answers to the big questions of life: Who are we? Why are we here? How should we live? But we are often unable to find the time or space to think positively and carefully about them.

At The Good Book Company, we're passionate about producing resources that help people of all ages and stages to understand the heart of the Christian message, found in the pages of the Bible, and to see how that message provides answers to our biggest questions.

So whoever you are and wherever you are at, we hope we can help you to think things through. Visit our website to discover the range of books and other resources we publish, both for people who are looking into Christianity and those who have already made the decision to follow Jesus. Or head to our partner site at christianityexplored.org/what-is-christianity for a clear explanation of who Jesus is and why he came.

Thanks again for reading.

Your friends at The Good Book Company

thegoodbook.com | thegoodbook.co.uk
thegoodbook.com.au | thegoodbook.co.nz

CHRISTIANITYEXPLORED.ORG
Our partner site is a great place to explore the Christian faith, with powerful testimonies and answers to difficult questions.